Presented to:

_____

From:

_____

Date:

_____

BE

20 WAYS TO EMBRACE
WHO YOU REALLY ARE

YOU

LISA LEONARD

FOUNDER OF
lisa leonard designs.®

ZONDERVAN®
.com

CONTENTS

INTRODUCTION

I grew up in a conservative Christian family in Orange County, California. I was one of seven children. With a tender heart and a desire to love others, I believed from a young age the most important thing about me was how I related to other people. I married a pastor who became a businessperson. Our first son, David, was born in 2002 with profound special needs. Matthias followed eighteen months later. I had dreamed of being a wife and mom since I was a little girl, so I poured my heart into creating a beautiful home and loving our boys. Perfection was the goal, and anything less was failure. Deep down, I questioned my value. If I was a good wife and mom, I was worthy of love. I could earn the right to take up space in the world. This fear of being unlovable drove my intense desire to love and serve. I loved my family, I wanted to serve my family, but I also needed to prove my worth. I was using good things in the wrong way. I was defensive anytime I made a mistake. I was tired and overwhelmed. My to-do list was never ending. I felt there weren't enough to-dos in the whole world that would make me lovable. I was already lovable, and I was already worthy, but I couldn't see it. I couldn't feel it.

I tried and tried to be good enough. I smiled when I felt sad, not wanting to inconvenience anyone with my feelings. When asked my preference, I shrugged, hoping it would simplify things if I didn't have an opinion. I tried to be needless and wantless. I slowly lost myself until I felt desperate and empty. Something had to change. I had to change.

It took time. It was messy. We went through a marriage crisis. We rebuilt our marriage with new rhythms, new ways of communicating. I stopped doing a lot of things and made space to think, feel, and just be alone with myself. I journaled and walked and napped. I grieved. Slowly I began to find myself again. I could feel my heart beating. I could think my own thoughts. I could sort through my own feelings— even the harder ones. I began to say what I wanted and needed—even if it was an inconvenience. I was beginning to see myself as a real person. Our marriage was made up of two people, and I was one of them. Our family was made up of four people, and I was one of them. I counted. I mattered. I needed to be me. It was hard and messy and the struggle was worth it. As I am learning to be me, I am able to love and serve others from a place of wholeness instead of trying to earn their love to fill a hole. I make mistakes, and I am able to see my imperfections, and I recognize I am still loved and worthy with all my flaws. As this truth roots itself deeply in my heart, it opens up space for me to have

room for other people's imperfections. We are imperfect people—and even in that place, we reflect the image of God. We are lovable. We are worthy. The God of the universe says so! In that place of honesty and weakness, I have found strength. As I have opened myself to feeling pain, I have found healing. As I have experienced the hard emotions of sadness and anger, I have made room for joy.

Perhaps you can relate to my journey. If you have questioned your worth and wondered deep down if you're lovable, then you're in the right place.

You matter.

You being *you* matters.

You were created to be you.

You are allowed to be you.

Let's explore together—finding our way to the truest, most beautiful part of you—your spark. Let's find our way to that deep knowing inside you—your soul, so very precious and loved by God.

Be you.

Be who *you* really are.

Even though it's messy,

complicated,

imperfect,

inconvenient.

Being you will enable you to love others better.

Being you will bring a fullness to you and those around you.

Being you won't be easy, but the journey will bring more peace and joy.

Being you is brave.

This is heart work.

This is soul work.

This is the most important work.

This is your work.

The world needs you to be you. The world needs you to be the person God created you to be—nothing more, nothing less. You.

Walk with me, and together we'll dig deep, push past fears, overcome darkness, and find something amazing: you. Step-by-step, day by day, each page of this book will help you on your journey to embracing who you really are. You—in all your messy, imperfect amazingness. Are you ready? Let's go.

BE
ENOUGH

I sat across the table from my dear friend, tears streaming down my face. "I don't know what's wrong with me," I said, trying to regain my composure. "The kids are healthy. I have an incredible husband. We have a beautiful home. Our business is thriving. I should be grateful, I should be joyful, but I feel miserable, empty, alone. I feel like nobody cares about me. What about my needs? Day after day I do the dishes, change the diapers, tidy the house, return the e-mails, take care of everyone. I'm tired. I need more than a nap, more than a pedicure once a month."

I tried so hard for so long to be the person I thought I was supposed to be. I tried to be selfless and set aside my own needs and wants. I tried to be happy when I felt sad, and patient when I felt angry. I tried to serve others—do more, be more. Wasn't that what love was? Serving others and being selfless? Wasn't that what a good wife and mom did—keep everything working smoothly, make everyone happy? Didn't all these things prove I was good at what I was responsible for? Didn't all these things prove I was worth loving?

I hoped I could find order, and in that order find safety, and in that safety find love. But I never found love there. With each smile,

I was losing myself. With each yes, I was disappearing a little. With each half-truth I was putting up a wall between me and those I loved. Eventually I ended up empty and desperate. I felt disconnected from my kids, my friends, my husband—the very people I so desperately wanted to connect with. Instead of order, everything seemed chaotic. Instead of safety, everything felt unstable. Instead of love, I felt loneliness. Instead of freedom, I felt weighed down. I was building a house of cards, and one small breeze would blow the whole thing over. I was losing my spark, lost in a fog of pleasing other people. My intentions were good, but here I was, in a coffee shop, with tears streaming down my face.

For so long my go-to responses had been, "I'm great!" "No problem." "It doesn't matter to me." "I'd love to help." "Don't worry about it!" I'd figure out what others wanted to hear, and that's what I would tell them. It felt easier, neater, and less complicated than the alternative.

Except I wasn't great.

And there was a problem.

It did matter to me.

I actually didn't want to help; I was already overwhelmed.

Maybe there was a reason to worry.

I started to see I wasn't being me. I wasn't showing up as my true self and being honest. I was putting on a mask and trying to become the person I thought I should be, the person I thought other people wanted me to be. I was building walls around myself and trying to control everyone and everything. I wasn't being honest. I was disappearing from my own life. I wanted to change, but how?

My friend was walking a similar journey, and her encouraging words spoke to my soul. I needed to be me. Me, in all my messy, imperfect amazingness. I needed space to think my thoughts, listen to my heart, make sense of my feelings, and pay attention to my thoughts. It had been so long since I had done any of these things that I hardly knew how to do them anymore.

I couldn't feel my feelings because I was so busy feeling everyone else's feelings. I needed space.

I couldn't think with all the noise. I needed quiet.

I couldn't breathe with all the busyness. I needed to slow down.

It would take some time to work my way back to me.

I know I'm not the only one who's felt this way. Day after day I meet incredible women who give everything they have to show up for their families and friends, and yet they feel exhausted and isolated. They feel like failures, as if they aren't enough. They wonder if they'll ever be enough. Maybe you feel this way too.

"I am enough"—it has become kind of a catchphrase, right? I see it on T-shirts, on wall canvases, on cards. The truth? We're not enough, and we know it deep down at our core. We are faced with our shortcomings on a daily, if not hourly basis. We're not just imperfect; sometimes we're downright mean and ugly. We're broken, and we suspect we'll always be broken.

I am not enough. You are not enough. It's like my soul knows it, your soul knows it. This feeling of not-enoughness is our default mode.

But.

But God.

God decided to love me. He decided to love you. He decided to love us despite our not-enoughness.

You don't have to do more to get His love.

You don't have to be the perfect wife and mom.

You don't have to smile when you feel sad or be patient when you feel angry.

Even if you stop doing good things, God will love you.

You didn't earn His love, and you can't lose His love.

When God decided to love you, He said, "You are enough."

You are lovable just as you are.

No more, no less. Just you, right now.

You don't have to be anything but *you.*

God decided to love me.
He decided to love you. He
decided to love us despite
our not-enoughness.

God made you just the way you are.

God loves you.

God wants you to be *you*.

This is our reality. With God, I am enough. You are enough.

But how do we live in this new reality? How do we live in the truth that we are loved *just as we are* by the God of the universe? How do we teach our souls to rest in the knowledge that *we are enough*—when every part of us feels like we're not?

Instead of looking through our own eyes, we need to look at ourselves with new eyes, the way God sees us—broken, yes, and still lovable.

You don't have to be more or less. You are allowed to fail. You are allowed to be imperfect. You are allowed to succeed. You are allowed to be amazing. You are allowed to feel whatever you feel.

You didn't do anything to earn this love, and you can't do anything to lose it.

You are enough right now

in this body,

with this face,

with that bad habit

and that bad mood.

You are enough right now,

in spite of what you've done.

No matter what you do,

it's not the doing
or undoing.
It just is.
You are enough right now
before time began,
after time ends,
in the slowness of long days
and the busyness of short days.
You are enough right now.
Breathe it in.
Hold this beautiful thought in your mind.
Let it fill you.
Let it soothe you.
You are enough right now.
You
are
enough.
Always have been,
always will be
loved
just as you are.

Fill in the blanks below.

Even when I

_____

   I am enough.

In spite of my

_____

   I am enough.

It's okay for me to feel

_____

   because I am enough.

I am

_____

   and I am enough.

Think on These Things

Today, find ten minutes for quiet. This time doesn't need to be fancy. Don't worry about doing it right. It doesn't have to be meditation or prayer. Set the timer, find a quiet spot to be alone, and just be with yourself. As you sit quietly, think about these words: I am enough, right here, right now. I don't have to do anything or be anything to be loved. I am loved. I am enough.

A Lie and a Truth

Write a lie you have believed about yourself.

Now cross it out and rewrite it as a true statement.

BE
OUT OF
CONTROL

*T*here are plenty of days when I feel like my to-do list is longer than the hours in the day or my energy level (whichever goes first, usually my energy level). David, our son with special needs, must be fed a special blended diet that's free of dairy, gluten, and soy, and he has to be diapered, bathed, and given medications multiple times each day. He also needs assistance and to be looked after all day, every day. Our younger son, Matthias, at fifteen years old, has completely different needs. He wants to talk about school and girls. He needs reminders about homework and chores. He needs time with us—playing and having fun. My relationship with my husband, Steve, requires time, nurturing, and attention. Housework is never ending. As soon as the dishes are done, they pile up again, and I'm fairly certain the laundry procreates at night while we're sleeping. Steve runs our jewelry-design business, but I am responsible for social media posts, creating new products, and being part of high-level strategy and planning. I often feel like the team is waiting for me to give them information or creative direction. Are you feeling stressed yet? I'm sure your to-do list is just as long and exhausting! Mine feels out of control. I feel out of control. And we haven't even looked at chores like car maintenance, doctor and

dentist visits, and scheduling the plumber. Life is crazy full, with more to do than can be done.

Up until a couple of years ago, I felt responsible not only for all these things, but also for making sure everyone in my family was happy, healthy, and generally in a good mood. If we had guests, it was my responsibility to make sure they slept well and had fun. Now, don't get me wrong, I want my family and friends to be happy, healthy, and well rested—but there is a difference between wanting good things for them and feeling personally responsible for their happiness. I thought I had to control everything and everyone. But I had a light-bulb moment a couple of years ago: I am one person. I am not God. I cannot control other people's thoughts and emotions. I had taken on an impossible task that would inevitably leave me feeling exhausted. I was doomed to fail. I could never be enough to be all those things to all those people—I wasn't designed for that role. I had taken on something that wasn't mine to take on, and I was tired of feeling like I wasn't enough.

So—the big questions: How did I let go of all that stress? How did I stop trying to manage other people's thoughts and feelings? How did I stop feeling like a failure and start believing I am enough—right here, right now?

It was a process. It took time and retraining. It took practice and patience—and I'm still learning. We'll go through a lot of steps in this book, and if you take the time to read, reflect, and practice what we cover here, your life and relationships will change.

We'll talk about making time for quiet, listening to your heart, nurturing your soul, believing other people are powerful, believing you are worth loving, and we'll talk about you being you in all your amazing youness. You are enough—right now. You don't need to do anything to be more loved. You don't need to stop doing anything to be more loved. You are loved in all your imperfect, incredible uniqueness.

Take a deep breath and journey with me on a path to letting life be whatever it is. Let life unfold and recognize you are not in control of most events and you're not in control of other people. You are simply one person, in this moment, showing up with a whole heart and loving yourself and others well.

Love doesn't mean making everything okay. Love doesn't mean controlling every circumstance and avoiding every difficulty. Love doesn't mean making other people happy. Love doesn't mean worrying endlessly and hoping it will change the outcome. Love means you care deeply about someone else and you believe they are powerful and able to deal with whatever life brings. Love means being in a healthy relationship with someone else with healthy respect for each other. I am a whole person. You are a whole person. I have needs just as you do, and my needs matter just like yours.

As humans, we are multifaceted and complex. We feel the spectrum of feelings—from elation to desperation. Sometimes we win, sometimes we lose, but most of the time it's somewhere in the middle. We take two steps forward and one step back—and that's okay. Giving ourselves

Love doesn't mean
making everything
okay. . . . Love means
you care deeply about
someone else and you
believe they are powerful
and able to deal with
whatever life brings.

space to be who we are means alleviating massive stress and pressure from our daily existence. Exhale. It's messy, it's beautiful, and here we are in the middle of it all.

Be tired and let yourself be tired.

Be grumpy and tell yourself it's okay to be grumpy.

Be wrong and own your mistake.

Be lazy and remind yourself downtime is necessary.

Be sick and take a sick day.

Be silly and laugh too loud.

Be happy and feel it from the tip of your toes to the top of your head.

Be messy and don't clean it up right away.

Be angry and take some time to breathe.

Be overwhelmed and lighten your schedule.

Be grateful and say thank you.

Be inspired and create something.

Be sad and admit this is really, really hard.

Be peaceful and soak up all the contentment.

Be content and be in the moment with all of its enoughness.

Slow down.

Breathe in, breathe out.
Slow down more.
Be you.
The world needs you
to be you,
and you need you
to be you.
You are enough.
You are loved.
You are worthy of good things.
Be you.

God is the One in control. God is the One who will take care of all the things weighing on your heart.

Another thing that works for me when things feel out of control is reminding myself that, yes, this feeling makes sense. I'm not in control. I don't have to be in control because God is in control.

Fill in the blanks below.

When

_____

I remind myself I'm not in control of that
situation.

When

_____

I remind myself I'm not in control of that
person.

When

_____

I remind myself I am not in control.

Think on These Things

I am responsible for me. I am not in control of others' thoughts and feelings. They are responsible for their own thoughts and feelings, and I am responsible for mine. I don't need to worry about everyone and everything.

A Lie and a Truth

Write a lie you have believed about yourself.

Now cross it out and rewrite it as a true statement.

BE
A WANNABE

DAY 3

*I*n seventh grade every student was required to take shop class. Half the semester was metal shop, and half the semester was wood shop. I remember my teacher seemed fairly apathetic, and I also remember there were a lot of saws, drills, fire, and heavy machinery. Even in my young, twelve-year-old mind, it seemed like a really bad combination.

One day, as we were all sitting around waiting for instructions, I overheard a couple of girls near me talking. "He's such a wannabe!" they said and laughed. They were talking about a boy sitting at another table. His name was Jeremy, and he was wearing Reebok tennis shoes. All I wanted in the world was Reebok tennis shoes. I thought if I could get Reeboks I would finally be cool. And here was Jeremy, wearing Reeboks and being called a "wannabe."

Oh my gosh, was I a wannabe?

"What's a wannabe?" I asked the girls.

"It's someone who wants to be cool," one of the girls replied.

I tried to process this information. *Wait. Don't these girls want to be cool too?* I thought. *Don't we all want to be cool?*

"He tries too hard," the other girl said.

I nodded and turned back around in my seat. I tried to absorb what

Aren't we all wannabes?
We want to be seen.
We want to matter.
We want to belong.
We want to be loved.

they were saying. *He wants to be cool, but he tries too hard. He's wearing Reeboks and he's still not cool.*

Was I trying too hard?

Weren't we all trying too hard—every single kid in our middle school? Weren't we all doing everything we could to be cool or at least not drown in the ocean of social pressure?

Wannabe. Aren't we all wannabes? We want to be seen. We want to matter. We want to belong. We want to be loved.

We are built with these desires—desires so deep it is instinctual from the moment we are born. For me, middle school was awful. I was deeply insecure, and I was certain everyone was laughing at me. If I caught a glimpse of myself in the locker room mirror, I would cringe. I couldn't stand the way I looked. I hated my frizzy, curly hair and the gap between my front teeth. I hated my fair skin. I hated the way I felt inside my skin. I wanted to be someone else. Someone cool, someone prettier, someone happier, someone more lovable.

I thought the answer was Reebok tennis shoes, but after this conversation I knew that wasn't the answer. Deep down I'd known that wasn't the answer—I just hoped the answer wouldn't be impossible to find.

I was a people pleaser trying to find myself in a sea of people. Who was I outside of other people? What did I think—even if it wasn't what my friends thought? How did I feel when I felt my own emotions instead of worrying about other people's emotions? Little by little I was growing and finding my own groove.

In the coming years I grew out my hair, got braces, developed a sense of style and a sense of self. I joined the swim team and got good grades. I loved youth group and felt a sense of belonging there. I made good friends who stood beside me and loved me. I stopped worrying if people were laughing at me. I was still a wannabe, still insecure, but I had found my people, my niche, my place. There was still a hole, but I found ways to fill it.

After college I married an amazing man, and we had two incredible boys. As family, business, and life became more demanding, I leaned into my people-pleasing ways. I put myself last, hoping that if everyone else was okay, maybe I would be okay too. I hoped if I made other people happy, they would love me. I wanted to be loved. I needed to be loved. But I thought I had to be someone else to be loved. I believed I was flawed, unlovable. My attempts to please others didn't work, and I ended up more desperate and lonely. I was trying so hard and doing it all wrong. It took time to get back to me. It took time to nurture myself, sit quietly, feel my feelings, and listen to my heart. It took time to get brave enough to speak my honest thoughts even if the person I was speaking to didn't like what I was saying. It took time journaling and meeting with a counselor. It took time letting go of worrying about what others thought of me. It took time to realize that when I am *me* in all my messy, amazing imperfection, I can love others well. When I let myself be flawed, silly, tired, creative, angry, inspired, quiet, sad, and curious, I am able to let other people be who they are.

I am learning to judge myself less harshly, to accept myself where I am, and to give that same love and acceptance to others.

I want to be me.

I want to be the *me* that God created me to be.

I want to be the best *me* I can be.

I never stopped being a wannabe. I still wannabe loved. I still try really hard—but now I focus that energy on being me.

I wannabe *me*.

And you wannabe you.

The world needs you to be you.

When I am *me* in all my messy, amazing imperfection, I can love others well.

Fill in the blanks below.

I want to be honest. I want to say

_____

I want to try new things, like

_____

I want to accept that I am

_____

I want to remind myself

_____

I want to love myself by

_____

I want to learn to

_____

I want to be *me*.

Think on These Things

I am me, just me. I don't have to be anything more or less. I don't have to be anyone else. I am me.

A Lie and a Truth

Write a lie you have believed about yourself.

Now cross it out and rewrite it as a true statement.

BE
BEAUTIFUL

A few summers ago, we had a big family vacation at a nearby lake. We rented a cabin, and we squished in to get time together with all the aunties, uncles, cousins, grandma, and grandpa. Between the afternoons swimming and the evenings making s'mores, my niece Clara mentioned she hated her teeth. I felt the same way when I was younger, so I wrote her this letter.

Until my sophomore year of high school, I had a gap between my front teeth too. Actually, it was a very large gap, and I was incredibly insecure about it. I tried to smile a smile that didn't show my teeth, but it was forced and awkward. Sometimes I would put a little piece of apple behind my front teeth, look in the mirror, and try to image how much more beautiful I would be if my teeth met in the middle.

I clearly remember one of my parents' friends telling me, "That gap is so large, you could drive a semi through it!" I'm sure he had no idea how sensitive I was about my teeth, but the comment stung. Even typing these words today, it still stings a little. Or I could tell you about the junior high boy who asked me if I was missing a tooth. I wanted to crawl under my desk and hide.

I was embarrassed. No, it was more than that. I was ashamed of the way I looked. I didn't want to be me.

Now I'm grown up, and I've had work done on my teeth. They line up perfectly, and there is no gap in the middle. I like my smile now, and I smile big for pictures without thinking about how my smile will look.

But I wish that I had known that I was beautiful then. Even with a gap between my teeth, I was lovely and valuable and amazing. Outward beauty isn't what makes a person beautiful or valuable or lovable.

I have known beautiful people who radiate kindness and love—who by the world's standards are unattractive. And I've known "perfect" and "popular" girls who are unkind and unhappy, and when I look at them, I don't see their shiny hair or perfect skin; all I see is unkindness. Yes, by the world's standards they may be beautiful, but it's hard to see past the rude comments and self-centeredness.

Can I tell you something, Clara? As you get older, you'll probably have your teeth fixed. You'll probably learn how to apply eye shadow so that it makes your blue eyes look even brighter than they already are. And you'll probably find the perfect pair of jeans that fit just right. But you will never be more beautiful than you are right now. Because what makes you beautiful is that you are you. You have a sweet and kind heart. You have a sparkle in your eye and a love for others. These things radiate out of you.

You are wonderfully made. Made to be YOU!

Even if you can't see it yet, you have to believe me. You are amazing and so incredibly special. It's not your teeth or your hair or how long your legs are that makes you lovely. It's just you, being you.

You are beautiful.

Deep down we believe if we can be pretty enough, smart enough, kind enough, and *good* enough, we will be lovable. But it's not true. We don't have to be anything or anyone other than who we are, right now. I am loved. You are loved.

Outward beauty isn't what
makes a person beautiful
or valuable or lovable.

Fill in the blanks below.

Having perfect

_____

won't make me more lovable.

Having better

_____

won't make me more worthy.

Even when I look

_____

I am lovable.

Think on These Things

I am beautiful because I am me. It's not the length of my legs or the style of my hair that makes me beautiful—it's the spark inside me that makes me beautiful. God gave me my very own spark. I am beautiful.

A Lie and a Truth

Write a lie you have believed about yourself.

Now cross it out and rewrite it as a true statement.

BE
AWKWARD

DAY 5

I was eighteen years old, sitting in one of my first classes at the conservative Christian university I attended. We sat in our chairs, lined up in rows. Everything was neat and tidy as our professor explained that day's class.

"Today we are going to discuss gray areas of our faith. Some people are comfortable with things that make others very uncomfortable. Because there are different interpretations of the Bible, there are parts of our faith we call 'gray areas' because they are not black-and-white. They are not neat and tidy. Does anyone have something they think of as a gray area?"

A young man near me spoke out first. "Alcohol," he said. "Most of the people at my church don't drink, while some enjoy a nice glass of wine with dinner. Drinking is a gray area."

We all laughed a little because our school was so conservative each of us had to sign an agreement we would not drink or dance while we attended. While drinking may be a gray area in most situations, it was black-and-white at our university.

"Excellent," our professor said. "What else?"

"Speeding on the freeway," said a girl across the room. "There is a

God can handle the ugliest stuff we bring before Him. It doesn't even faze Him—because He already knows the deepest parts of my heart.

posted speed limit, but most of us regularly exceed the speed limit, and it doesn't bother us. Officers don't usually pull a car over until they're going at least ten miles over the speed limit."

"Insightful," responded our professor. "What do other people think about speeding?"

We stayed on the topic of speeding for a few minutes—some feeling strongly there was nothing wrong with speeding, other arguing a posted speed limit was a clear boundary and should be heeded.

"Okay, what's another gray area?" my professor asked.

The room was quiet just long enough for me to get up the courage to speak.

"Cussing," I said.

"Cussing? How so?" asked my professor.

"Well . . ." I paused, considering how to respond, "is it wrong to feel like s***, or just to say you feel like s***?"

The room was completely silent. It was like time had stopped. The tension was so thick I could cut it with a knife.

I must be dreaming, I thought, trying to wake myself up.

Wake up.

Wake up.

But no, I was not dreaming. I was sitting in the middle of my university course, all eyes wide, tension filling the air. I felt my cheeks turn red and realized I was the only one who thought cussing was a gray area. And I had just said the word s*** *twice*.

The professor cleared his throat. "Umm, okay," he said tentatively. "Does anyone else have thoughts on cussing?"

The rest of the class was a blur except I know for certain no one agreed with me. Cussing was not a gray area. It was black-and-white.

After what seemed like forever, the class finally ended. I grabbed my bag and left as quickly as I could. Back in the safety of my dorm room, I didn't know whether to laugh or cry. I think I did both.

How humiliating! Oh. My. Gosh. Did I really just say s*** *twice* in my college class?

I lay down on my bed to process what is likely one of my most embarrassing moments.

Is it wrong to feel like s***? I don't know.

Is it wrong to *say* you feel like s***? Yes, most definitely *yes*.

I sat with this for a minute and realized, I disagreed.

I believe it's okay to say, "I feel like s***."

God can handle the ugliest stuff we bring before Him. It doesn't even faze Him—because He already knows the deepest parts of my heart.

And He loves me.

When I feel sad, God says, "Come to Me; let Me hold you."

When I feel angry, God can handle it. He isn't surprised or offended.

When I feel overjoyed, God celebrates with me.

When I am suffocated by that thing I've done, the one that covers mc in shame, God says, "I already know all about it. You are Mine and I love you."

Whatever I think, whatever I feel, no matter how crass or rude or mean or ugly, I can feel it. I can say it. I can name it. The God of the universe opens His arms to me.

Even when the situation is not neat and tidy. Maybe especially when it's not neat and tidy. Perhaps it's in the mess that we get to see God's grace most clearly.

Those were awkward moments that day in class, but I'm so proud of my eighteen-year-old self for speaking truth. I was speaking into something much bigger than I realized at the time. I was asking, "Is it okay to be me—with all the messy, ugly, dark parts of myself, or do I need to wear a mask and pretend to be someone else?" In that room the silence answered my question. The silence said, "Hide those ugly, messy, dark parts of yourself." But it was too late. I had let out the truth. I had asked a hard question and received a hard answer. It was up to me to decide at that point: *Will I be me, or will I hide?* It's taken years of back and forth, up and down, forward and back, but I'm leaning into the wisdom of that eighteen-year-old girl. It's okay to feel what you feel, and it's okay to say what you feel. Be you. Be you in all your messy, amazing imperfection.

Fill in the blanks below.

Even when it's awkward I can

_____

I can feel

_____

even if it makes someone else uncomfortable.

Sometimes I'm awkward. Sometimes I

_____

And that's okay.

Think on These Things

I can say what I really think even if it's awkward. I can say what I really feel even if it's uncomfortable. I can be me in all my messy, amazing awkwardness.

A Lie and a Truth

Write a lie you have believed about yourself.

Now cross it out and rewrite it as a true statement.

BE
A CLIMBER

I was done. My boyfriend and I argued late into the night. After hours of negotiating and tears, we broke up. No matter how hard I tried to help him climb out of the mess he was in, it never worked. I wanted out.

Once the relationship was over, I was sad, but also relieved. I had stayed with him for almost two years of chaos and drama, and I was exhausted. I had been so busy trying to save him that I didn't realize how much of myself I'd lost along the way. In the days and weeks that followed, life began to feel brighter and lighter. I had more energy to focus on my own life. *Why was I so determined to hold his ladder when I had my own ladder to climb?*

I started spending time with my girlfriends again, something I loved but had stopped doing while we were dating. He hated country music, so after we broke up, I started listening to country music—and to this day I still love it. I redid my bedroom, painting the walls a bright yellow and covering the bed with a vintage cream cover. I focused renewed energy on my job, which I had been neglecting. I also spent more time hanging out with my closest friends.

Eventually, I heard through mutual friends that my ex was doing better. Now that I was out of his life, he was taking responsibility for himself and getting the help he needed. He had found his ladder. It was a long time before I realized that my efforts to help him—to hold his ladder—were actually hindrances. How could he take responsibility for his life when I was so determined to take responsibility for him? He couldn't get to his ladder because I was blocking it. The more I tried to help, the worse things became. He didn't need me to hold his ladder; he could climb it on his own. Or not. But either way, it was never my ladder to begin with.

I wish I could say that was the last time I tried to hold someone else's ladder, but it wasn't. In fact, it's a lesson I'm still learning, slowly but surely. I have my own ladder to climb—a sturdy and stable ladder that will take me where I need to go. We all have our own ladders, the rungs we need to climb to grow and move forward in life. Every rung requires bravery. I can cheer for a friend or my sister or my husband. I can encourage my kids as they go higher, rung by rung. When someone I love is struggling, I can speak words of love and truth. I can remind them that they are capable and brave.

But I cannot hold their ladders—and they cannot hold mine. When I tried to hold my boyfriend's ladder, not only was I not climbing my own ladder, but I was getting in his way. We each have our own ladder to climb. We each have a deep knowing inside us to guide us as we make our way through life. It's a journey each of us must make on our own. And most importantly, I'm learning we each have the power to do it.

When someone I love is struggling, I can speak words of love and truth. I can remind them that they are capable and brave.

Fill in the blanks below.

I climb my own ladder when I

_____

I want to get out of the way. I want to believe

_____

    can climb their own ladders.

I can cheer others on and encourage them to
climb their own ladder by

_____

Think on These Things

I have my own ladder to climb—this is what God has for me. Others have their own ladders to climb—this is what God has for them. I am powerful and capable, just as the ones I love are powerful and capable.

A Lie and a Truth

Write a lie you have believed about yourself.

Now cross it out and rewrite it as a true statement.

BE
CURIOUS

The day my first son, David, was born was one of the hardest days of my life. I was overwhelmed with what was in front of us. Our lives were forever changed. We now had a baby with only two fingers on his left hand and many other special needs—both physical and cognitive. Grief took me apart. This extreme, soul-breaking grief put an end to the old and brought with it the beginning of the new. What was, was no longer. What was to be was unknown. In my grief, I was faced with my complete lack of control and understanding. There was no faking it.

Grief took away all my defenses and ripped away the mask I wore. It left me exposed and naked. It was a kind of starting over. I began again, step by tiny step. Wake up. Brush teeth. Put on clothes. Eat something. Small actions required extreme effort because I was learning them again, learning everything again in the face of the new unknown.

We were undone. We were taken apart suddenly, and very, very slowly God was putting us back together. But we were not the same as we were before.

I remembered the girl I used to be. I used to laugh. I used to be carefree. But that was before my son was born with a severe disability, before my baby was born with two fingers, before the world stopped turning. I doubted I would ever laugh or feel carefree again.

We were taken apart suddenly,
and very, very slowly God was
putting us back together.

For the first few weeks of David's life, time slowed to a crawl. The minutes seemed to drag on and on. Weeks felt like months, and months felt like years. It seemed I could live lifetimes in my grief.

Why? Why? Why?

For weeks, the question circled my brain like a forgotten record spinning round and round.

Over and over I asked, "Why? Why does our baby have a disability? Why is this happening to us? Why God?"

For a while it seemed like my questions fell into an empty void. Did I even believe in God? Was He real? Did He love me? Why would God allow this pain? Yes, I believed in God. I did not understand what was happening, but I believed the God of the universe loved me. I believed He loved David.

"Then why? If You love me, if You love my baby, why?"

God spoke to my heart, not with words, not with an answer exactly, but with a soothing calm. *I am giving you a gift. Just trust Me*, He whispered.

The doctors told us David had a syndrome called Cornelia de Lange.

"He'll never walk or talk. He will be severely retarded," they told us.

"A gift? This doesn't feel like a gift, but I believe You are God," I whispered. "I'm confused. Nothing makes sense. Help me, God. Help me to see the gift in this pain."

I was undone. For the first three weeks of David's life, we went home every evening while our baby slept in the neonatal intensive care unit (NICU) at the hospital a couple of miles from our apartment. Parents were not permitted in the NICU during the daily staff change when the day staff left and the night shift arrived. I wanted to be with David twenty-four hours a day while he was in the NICU, but we were tired. We needed to eat. We needed to sleep. It was torture for me. My heart broke as we said goodbye and kissed David's tiny forehead at 7:00 every evening. We walked to our car without our son. Our arms were empty when they should have been full with our baby, diaper bag, and car seat. Every evening as we left the hospital, we drove past a big oak tree. It seemed so solid and unchanging when our lives were completely upended.

And every evening I prayed, "Please, God, comfort my baby when I cannot be there. Hold him and nurture him while he sleeps in his incubator. Give my baby what I cannot give him."

We moved through the motions of our days in the NICU. We held David, changed his diapers, and practiced feeding him through a tube running through his nose into his stomach. David's room at our apartment was all ready for him, but it had been prepared for a different baby. Inside the dresser drawers were clothes washed and folded for an eight-pound baby. We didn't have one item of clothing that would fit our tiny David. The car seat needed to be adjusted to the smallest setting, and even then we would need to tuck blankets around David to keep him secure. The newborn diapers wouldn't fit him for another four months. We were as physically unprepared for the arrival of our new baby as we were emotionally.

"A gift? This doesn't feel like a gift, but I believe You are God."

One afternoon, I stepped outside the NICU with a folder of bills and the checkbook. Even in crisis, real life demands to be lived. Bills had to be paid. Cars needed gas. Dishes had to be washed.

This is so strange, I thought. *Who cares about the gas bill? My baby was born with two fingers on his left hand.*

Just like that big oak tree next to the hospital, the outside world seemed unchanged. It felt surreal to do normal, everyday tasks while our world crumbled around us. As I wrote the first check and tucked it inside the envelope, our friends Josh and Maggie walked into the lobby. In the early years of our marriage, they had been our upstairs neighbors, worked in ministry with us, and became some of our closest friends. They joined me on the uncomfortable lobby couch and said nothing. They just sat, no words. I set the bills aside, buried my head

in my hands, and began to sob. The tears seemed to come from a bottomless well inside me. As I gave in to the grief, I wondered if I would ever stop crying. I held the pain in all its unbearable heaviness. Josh and Maggie sat with me and cried with me, holding me in their arms. They were powerless to change the situation, but they stepped inside the darkness with me. I wasn't alone.

I was learning pain demanded to be felt. It wouldn't be rushed. It wouldn't be pushed away or minimized. There was no set timeline for our grief. There were no Bible verses or life truths that could lessen pain's grip. No matter how much I wanted to push it away or pretend it wasn't there, there were no tricks or tips to lessen the agony. Josh and Maggie knew that I needed to honor my pain by acknowledging its heaviness and hurt, by allowing it to wash over me like a tidal wave— and that only in its own time would that pain begin to recede bit by bit. At that moment, the only thing I could do was grieve, not knowing if hope would ever come.

Josh and Maggie honored my pain. They honored our tiny baby David and the difficult road ahead of him. They honored our broken hearts and lost dreams. They didn't minimize the journey before us with advice or easy answers. They loved David exactly as he was—a whole soul inside a broken body. I didn't know it yet, but my tears were making room for joy. God was using the ache to stretch and grow my heart to make room for a deeper love. God was going to use this grief to help me stretch and grow. He was going to use David to teach me how to be *me*.

Fill in the blanks below.

It's okay to ask God, "Why?" One situation that confuses me is

_____

There is room for pain and hurt. I make space for these feelings by

_____

I am stretching and growing to make room for

_____

Think on These Things

I can be curious. I can ask God, "Why?" God can handle my questions, my doubt, my heartache. I am stretched most when life is hardest. I grow in the mess of life. God uses the hardest stuff in life to help me become me.

A Lie and a Truth

Write a lie you have believed about yourself.

Now cross it out and rewrite it as a true statement.

BE
RESTED

I have undervalued rest and quiet. I've pushed myself and pushed myself past exhaustion, not getting enough sleep, and felt as though I had to keep going. Eventually this would lead to a breakdown.

Steve started a new pastor job at a new church in a new town when David was eighteen months old and I was thirty-eight weeks pregnant with Matthias. Matthias was born twelve days after we moved in. We were mostly unpacked, and the boys' room was set up with matching cribs. We were in a massive transition with two tiny babies.

Right after we moved to town, we met one of the most amazing families I've ever known—the Keeters. They loved us from the beginning, and their daughter Ali would become one of our favorite babysitters and basically a lifesaver.

One day, Ali came over to watch the boys, and I went into my bedroom and crawled into bed. I planned to rest for a minute, but I fell into a deep sleep for two hours. While Ali fed the boys, played with them, and rocked them, I slept. I woke up disoriented.

Oh my gosh! I just slept for two hours! In the middle of the day! I just took an eighteen-dollar nap!

Money was tight. We didn't have eighteen dollars to waste on a nap!

I should have been productive during those two hours. Instead I not only wasted time; I wasted money. I felt so guilty.

When Steve got home that evening, I told him how guilty I felt. He hugged me and said, "Babe. You must have needed the sleep. That's probably the best eighteen dollars we've spent lately."

Wait. Really?

I mattered? Rest mattered? I deserved to sleep?

It was not only okay—it was important.

The dishes could wait; the laundry could wait. (Actually, Ali probably folded it while I was sleeping!) This mama needed sleep. I was up with the boys the night before, and I would likely be up with them again that night.

Rest. Exhale. Soak it up.

It's good. It matters. You matter.

You being your best you matters

You being rested matters. Even if it costs eighteen dollars (or more).

Rest.

Nap.

Sleep in.

Take a walk.

Let the sun warm your shoulders.

Sit quietly.

Hire a sitter.

Soak in the tub.

Go away overnight by yourself.
Sip hot tea, and then make another cup, and take your time.
Make a new recipe.

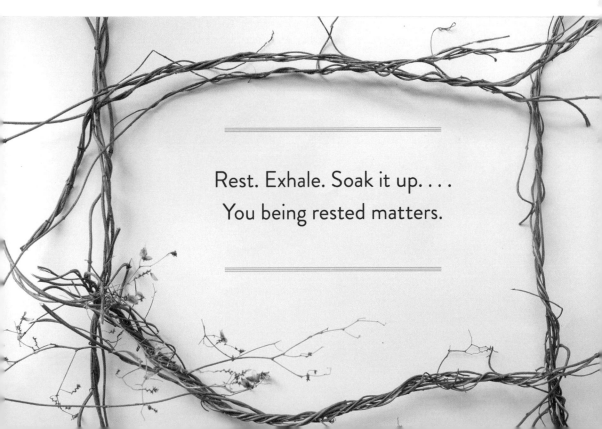

Rest. Exhale. Soak it up. . . .
You being rested matters.

Fill in the blanks below.

I need rest. I need time to think. I need

_____

Three things that give my soul rest are

_____

_____

_____

Sometimes rest means saying no. It's okay for
me to say no to

_____

Think on These Things

I need sleep. I need rest. I need to make sleep a priority. I am worthy of rest.

A Lie and a Truth

Write a lie you have believed about yourself.

Now cross it out and rewrite it as a true statement.

BE
GENEROUS

*W*hen the boys were little, Steve was on staff at a church we attended. There was a tradition where parents of children in the church nursery took turns working in the nursery. I thought this was a fantastic idea. I love children—both mine and other people's, and I would have loved to help take care of them one Sunday morning a month. There was just one little problem. I was exhausted and overwhelmed. I was spent. I had two small children, one with significant special needs, and I didn't have anything left to give. I was emotionally and physically worn-out caring for my own kiddos. Sunday was a time I could put them in the nursery and sit quietly in church. I needed that downtime.

I would happily serve somewhere else in the church. I could bring a meal to a family in crisis. I could help set up the coffee station. I could make a necklace for a new mom. I could arrange flowers for a special church family dinner. I would even help set up chairs before service with a baby strapped to my chest. I just couldn't rock someone else's baby in the nursery. I couldn't change another child's diaper. I wanted to be generous, but I needed a break from childcare. And you know what? That was okay. When I finally told our nursery director, she was gracious. She reminded me there were other people who could fill the

Being generous blesses both
the giver and the receiver. But
that doesn't mean we can be
generous in every area.

need besides me. There were other people who had energy to work in the nursery and lavish attention on the little ones.

We are made to be generous, and I believe our hearts grow and expand as we give to others. Being generous blesses both the giver and the receiver. But that doesn't mean we can be generous in every area.

Maybe you'll be the PTA president at your child's school. Or maybe you'll be the mom who isn't very involved on your child's school campus.

Maybe you'll work the sound system at church.

Maybe you'll write encouraging notes to friends who are struggling.

Maybe you'll pray faithfully for your friends and family.

Maybe you'll lead mission trips.

Maybe you'll sing onstage to help lead worship.

Maybe you'll make the perfect chocolate chip cookies for a big gathering.

Maybe you'll be a dedicated nursery worker for decades, or maybe you'll serve somewhere else.

We each have unique gifts to give. They may be big or small, but they are important. Be generous with others, and don't forget to be generous with yourself. Speak kind words to others and to yourself. Give where you're able to give yourself freely, and give yourself grace when you're not able to give in certain areas.

Fill in the blanks below.

I have gifts to give. One gift I love to give is

_____

One area where I am cautious about giving is

_____

I feel like I was made to serve by

_____

Think on These Things

I am generous with myself and others. I love to give gifts of time, attention, kind words, and service, as I am able. I am careful to nurture my own heart so I am able to be generous with myself and others.

A Lie and a Truth

Write a lie you have believed about yourself.

Now cross it out and rewrite it as a true statement.

BE
CREATIVE

I 'm not creative."

I regularly hear people say this.

Sure, maybe you don't draw or paint or create clay sculptures, but I promise you, you are creative. You were created by the Creator to create! It's part of our humanity. But creativity is scary and hard. If it matters to us, then it's vulnerable.

What does your creativity look like? It could be cooking, gardening, putting together fun outfits, cutting hair, decorating, taking cell phone pictures, playing a musical instrument, organizing, flower arranging, dancing, singing, or acting. There are a million ways to be creative. Your heart wants to create. Your heart wants to bring beauty into the world. You were made for this!

Years ago, when I was beginning to make jewelry, I sent a couple of samples to one of my favorite local boutiques. The shop was located near the beach and carried high-end clothing, vintage décor, and handmade jewelry. I followed up with a phone call, and we scheduled a time to meet. The thought of having my handmade creations in her store was exhilarating. It was exciting and humbling. It was also terrifying.

I carefully chose some of my favorite creations—lots of necklaces and a few earrings. Each piece was placed in an individual box, and all the boxes were gathered into a structured bag. On the day of our meeting, I loaded up my creations, found a parking space near the boutique, and walked with trembling steps through the door.

Deep breath.

The owner smiled and welcomed me to her shop. We chatted about the beautiful weather outside and a new label she was carrying in her store. As we talked, I began to lay out each necklace side by side. As I laid out the handmade pieces, I felt like I was laying out my soul, baring some of my most vulnerable hopes and dreams.

She turned her attention from the conversation to the handmade jewelry in front of her. With the precision of a surgeon and the strong opinions of an experienced buyer, she began to separate the necklaces into two categories. She went through each piece and decided whether or not it suited her taste. I could feel her words cut through me.

Yes.

No.

No.

Yes.

No.

Yes.

With each no my heart sank a little lower, and I wished the ground would swallow me up. With each yes my hopes were boosted slightly.

Creativity requires
courage.

I felt like a Ping-Pong ball—*she liked it, she hated it, she liked it, she hated it.*

After a few very short minutes that felt like an eternity, she counted the yes necklaces, pulled out her checkbook, and paid me for the pieces. I thanked her, packed up the rejected necklaces, walked outside, and got in my car. I drove down the street and pulled into a quiet parking spot. Then, like every strong and capable entrepreneur, I burst into tears. I felt humiliated. I felt rejected. I felt stupid. Who did I think I was making handmade jewelry? I was a failure.

But I could hear a little voice reminding me that this shop, a shop I loved, was carrying some of my handmade designs. Sure, she didn't like every piece, but she liked some of them. She was carrying my

designs. It was a success, not a failure. And even if she hadn't bought one single necklace, that didn't mean I was a failure either. It only meant the jewelry wasn't to her taste.

I was beginning to understand that creativity requires courage. The jewelry was part of me. In a very real way, it was an expression of my heart.

Creativity is like hopping across a rocky stream, jumping from one stone to the next. Watching someone else do it is easy. But as I took my first leap, my foot landed on a slightly unstable stone. Should I jump to the next stone or turn back? I could see the next stone, so I jumped. In order to get across the stream, I had to jump one stone at a time—sometimes changing course. I had to be brave.

Each step takes me further on my journey and provides new opportunities, new insights, and new challenges. With each leap I am learning new ways of thinking that had never crossed my mind before. With each leap I am getting braver.

But how do we find courage to leave the shore? How do we find the bravery to jump from one stone to the next? I've found a few simple but profound truths that work for me.

1. I believe I am worthy and loved no matter what. My value isn't determined by a successful jewelry business. I am enough. If I fail, I will still be loved. I will still be precious. I am surrounded by family and friends who treasure me just because I am *me*. Even when I land on a shaky stone, I have a solid foundation. This gives me courage—so much courage!

2. I separate my art from my soul—at least a bit. The work of my hands is a reflection of me, but it's not *me*. When someone doesn't like my jewelry, that doesn't mean they are rejecting me. It simply means they don't like my jewelry. And that's okay. But in the rare circumstance where they are rejecting me? Well, I go back to number one—I am worthy and loved no matter what.

3. Failure is one of the best ways to learn. It's impossible to succeed all the time. If I'm able to look at a failure head-on, knowing it doesn't define me, I can learn from it, change a few things, and forge ahead. Failure can be my friend.

Fill in the blanks below.

Creativity is vulnerable. Something I've been wanting to try is

_____

I feel like a failure in this creative area:

_____

I can give myself permission to try and fail at

_____

Think on These Things

I am made to create. I use my creativity to nurture my soul. I use my creativity as a gift to others. When I am being creative, I am being me. I don't have to create perfect things—some of the things I create are amazing and some are not so amazing. As I create, I reflect God as Creator.

A Lie and a Truth

Write a lie you have believed about yourself.

Now cross it out and rewrite it as a true statement.

BE
HONEST

I've always considered myself an honest, kind person. But in order to be kind, I couldn't be completely honest. If I told people what I really thought, I would hurt their feelings. If I said what I really wanted, it would complicate things. If I said what I really felt, it would overwhelm people. So I was honest but not completely honest. I wasn't even completely honest with myself. Some of those thoughts, feelings, wants, and needs felt so ridiculously huge and selfish that I couldn't even admit them to myself.

I wanted to be kind. I wanted to be selfless. I wanted to make others happy.

But with each passing moment, I was disappearing. It happened slowly—so slowly I didn't even realize it was happening. I kept pushing down all those thoughts, feelings, needs, and wants, and I truly believed if I could make my family and friends happy, I would find the peace and joy I so desperately wanted. Deeper down beyond that, I believed their thoughts, feelings, needs, and wants were more important than my own.

I could be needless and wantless. That was love, right? Wrong.

It all came to a head a couple of years ago. I was empty and desperately sad, and I didn't know why. I had been ignoring my thoughts and feelings for so long that I couldn't make sense of the emotional turmoil inside me. All I knew was I couldn't take it anymore. Something had to change. I had to change. Everything had to change.

I had to tell my husband, Steve, I wanted to separate. I felt like I was walking away from my family, my friends, and my faith.

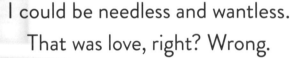

I could be needless and wantless.
That was love, right? Wrong.

We drove separately to our counselor's office and met up in the parking lot. When I saw Steve, I wanted to run over and hug him. I wanted to comfort him and tell him everything would be okay. But I didn't run to him, and I didn't comfort him. For so long I tried to make everything okay, but nothing was okay. I was about to communicate one of the hardest things I've ever had to say. I tried to find the anger and desperation deep inside me and hold on to those feelings. I tried to remember why I wanted to separate. Perhaps if we took some time apart I could find myself again. Perhaps if we didn't see each other for a while we could start to see each other again—not just with our eyes but with our hearts. Perhaps we could pause and then start over. Perhaps next time we could do things differently.

We walked up the steps to our counselor's office, and I was consumed by a feeling of dread. It was a weight so heavy I thought I might crumble underneath it.

I loved Steve. I hated him. I wanted to be with him. I wanted to run away. I wanted to scream. I wanted to cry. I wanted him to hold me. I didn't want him to touch me.

I didn't know what I wanted.

I wished I could be anywhere but here.

We sat side by side on a love seat in the counselor's office. This wasn't our regular counselor—she had canceled our appointment because she was sick. But I couldn't wait any longer. I couldn't go one more day without sharing my heart—the deepest, darkest, scariest stuff. It was time.

So there we sat, next to each other, but we did not touch. We knew each other so well, but we felt like strangers. We were still a couple; would we be a couple after this? We were together, but would we be together after I told Steve what I had to say? I felt as if I was standing on the edge of a cliff, about to jump off. I was terrified. This was the hardest thing I had ever done.

"Lisa," the counselor said, "is there something you want to tell Steve?"

"Yes," I said, trying to keep my voice steady. I felt like my throat was closing, but I willed the words to come. I wanted to run out of the room. I wanted the ground to swallow me up. I wanted to call the whole thing off.

But I didn't run. The ground didn't swallow me up. I didn't call the whole thing off. I leaped off the cliff not knowing what the future held. I left what was known behind me and hurdled into the unknown.

"Steve, I think we need to separate," I said.

The words were out there—in the real world. They hung in the air, and time seemed to stand still. I simultaneously wished I could take them back and felt relieved that I had actually said them out loud.

The look on Steve's face was a mix of confusion and desperation. I felt my heart breaking for him. I hated this—but I couldn't see any other way.

"What?" he asked.

"I think we need some time apart," I said again. "I need some time to think and figure things out."

The universe cracked into pieces, and the world fell apart. Steve was crying. I was crying. My head was spinning. I couldn't think or hear or see straight. It was like I had left my body. I felt numb.

The counselor was talking to Steve now. Everything was blurry, loud, confusing, and absolutely terrifying. It felt so dark in this new unknown place. I had jumped off the cliff, and I was falling through the air. Would I fall forever? Was I about to crash into the hard earth? What would the future hold?

In these darkest moments, when I felt like I was walking away from my faith, my family, my friends, God met me with an intense feeling of, *Now you're getting somewhere, Lisa. Now you're being honest. Now, the real growth and change is about to begin.*

The days and weeks that followed were hard. I was disoriented, walking through darkness, trying to find my way. I was hurting; Steve was hurting. I wanted to make it better for him, but first I needed to find clarity for myself. I needed space to think and breathe and just be. Things got messier before they got better, but eventually they did get better. We came back together. We were gentle with each other. We took our time. We built new routines. We made change. It was so hard but so worth it. Today our relationship is stronger than it's ever been.

Fill in the blanks below.

One of the scariest things for me to admit is

_____

I try to protect others' feelings by

_____

I am learning to be honest about

_____

Think on These Things

I can be honest no matter how messy and dark and awful. I am loved even in the midst of this messy darkness. No matter how big my mistakes, how big the mess, God meets me there with love.

A Lie and a Truth

Write a lie you have believed about yourself.

Now cross it out and rewrite it as a true statement.

BE
QUIET

L *ife is crazy busy, and it often feels as if I'm rushing from one thing to the next. Quiet would be nice, but it's not realistic. After all, I've got two boys, one with significant special needs, who need my attention. I can't keep up as it is—my e-mail in-box is overflowing, the house is messy, and there are piles of laundry waiting to be folded. Quiet and rest are a luxury I can't afford. I simply can't justify it.*

This is how I used to think. Rest was a luxury—something to be earned after every item on my to-do list was checked off, which rarely happened. So, if I took time for quiet or rest, I was taking something I didn't deserve.

A couple of years ago I kept coming across people who recommended making space for quiet. I saw a couple of Instagram posts about it, I stumbled across an article in a magazine, and while we were having coffee together, a friend mentioned needing space for quiet. It sounded wonderful, but how? Isn't making space for quiet self-indulgent? What about all the tasks that needed doing? My husband, Steve, told me about a book he was reading called *Rest* by Alex Soojung-Kim Pang. In the book he talks about making space for quiet, for rest, for downtime—and how it actually makes us *more* productive.

What? Could this be true? It seemed so counterintuitive. But I was drawn to the idea. I felt exhausted all the time and often discouraged. Every day brought more to do, and I was tired of the grind. I felt like I was taking care of everyone else, but no one was taking care of me. Something had to change.

I decided to take ten minutes to sit quietly on the couch—no cell phone, no music, just me sitting on the couch in silence. I set the timer and sat down. I took a deep breath and looked around the room.

I should really clean the TV. It's filthy, I thought.

Nope, just gonna sit here until the timer goes off.

I felt drawn to my phone. I wanted to scroll through Instagram, look at inspiration on Pinterest, something to pass the time. I felt bored and jumpy.

I glanced at the timer on my phone—nine minutes to go.

Why did this feel so strange? Sitting still with my thoughts wasn't something I did regularly, but I wanted to experiment. I kept at it.

I looked around the room.

I looked at my hands.

I paid attention to my thoughts.

I paid attention to my feelings.

Finally the timer went off and the ten minutes were up.

During that ten minutes, nothing happened. I didn't have any light-bulb moments. I didn't feel a sense of calm wash over me. I just felt bored and fidgety. But there was a part of me that wanted to do it again. The next day I set my timer for ten minutes and sat on the couch quietly.

And nothing happened again, except I kind of liked it.

After a few days of sitting quietly on the couch for ten minutes daily, I felt myself thinking more clearly. It was like my brain had time to reorganize itself. I felt less confused, less muddled about my feelings. I was beginning to have some clarity. This didn't happen during the ten minutes on the couch. It happened outside of that time. The ten minutes of quiet was a catalyst for me. It was helping my brain work better. It was giving me space to actually think and feel instead of rushing around avoiding thinking and feeling.

When I speak to groups, I am often asked the question, "If I want to make change in my life, how do I start?"

My answer is, "Make space for ten minutes of quiet every day."

I don't mean time for reading your Bible or praying or meditating (although if you want to pray or meditate, feel free!). It doesn't have to be fancy or perfect.

I also warn people when I recommend quiet. If you make space to be alone with your thoughts and feelings, things will happen. We are so busy—and part of why we stay so busy is to avoid our thoughts and feelings. We want to avoid things that are uncomfortable. It's difficult to look the truth in the face. *What do I actually think? What do I actually feel?* Making space for quiet is brave. It will lead to change. You will begin to have insights about next steps for change in your life. You will begin to see more clearly the things you like and don't like. Making change is hard, but the results are empowering.

Make space for quiet.

Make space to be still.

Make space to listen to your heart.

Make space to feel your feelings.

Make space for tears and laughter and anger.

Make space to think your thoughts without interruption.

Make space to let your mind wander.

Make space to notice the birds chirping outside.

Make space to rest for a bit.

Make space to breathe in and out.

Make space to slow down and stop rushing.

Make space to relax your shoulders.

Make space to be a person who needs space.

Make space for you to be you in all your messy amazingness.

If you make space to
be alone with your
thoughts and feelings,
things will happen.

Fill in the blanks below.

Sometimes I avoid quiet by filling the space with

_____

It's difficult to make space for quiet because

_____

One way I can carve out space for quiet is

_____

Think on These Things

I need space. I need quiet. I need time to think and feel and process. This time is not wasted—these are actually some of the most important moments of my day.

A Lie and a Truth

Write a lie you have believed about yourself.

Now cross it out and rewrite it as a true statement.

BE
STRETCHED

A few months ago, Steve and I headed to Washington, DC, to do a morning show for his lifestyle brand, Stephen David Leonard. While we were there, we hosted a gathering with friends and community members at Barnes and Noble, ate lots of really good food, and planned in some downtime to see the sites. I'd never been to Washington, DC, and I loved it! It has a unique vibe of politics, history, and culture.

As we were walking the city, we noticed all kinds of people riding electric scooters. I'd heard about cities launching electric scooter programs (download app, punch in credit card info, and ride off!), but this was the first time I'd seen scooters around a city. It looked like so much fun!

"Babe, we should totally get scooters!" I said. I imagined us scooting around the Lincoln monument with the wind in our hair and smiles on our faces.

We each downloaded the app, put in our credit card info, and got ready to ride off on our scooters. Steve hopped on his easily and started down the street. I tried to get on but felt unsteady. I didn't want to punch it and go too fast. I wasn't sure how to brake, and I really didn't want to fall, but mostly I felt wobbly and *so nervous.*

"Hang on, babe," I said, sweating and shaking.

"Take your time, sweetie," he said. "Hold on to the handlebar like this so you can brake easily." He showed me with his thumb extended.

"Just let me figure this out. Don't try to help," I said, frustrated and feeling stupid.

Why am I so nervous? I thought. *This should be easy. It looks so easy.*

I finally got kicked off and hopped on the scooter. It started to move forward slowly, but after five feet there was a couple walking on the sidewalk, and I got nervous and jumped off.

"Grrrrr!!" I felt angry. I hated this. *Scooters are stupid.*

"Babe, forget this," I said. "I want to stop."

"Hang in there, sweetie," Steve said patiently. "Let's find a quieter street so you can practice."

I was not having fun. I was not feeling the wind through my hair. I was not smiling.

I felt shame.

Why can't I be more athletic? Why are things like this so hard for me?

I walked along the sidewalk with my scooter, feeling like I might burst into tears.

I'd try to kick off, scoot for a few feet, and then freak out and jump off while the scooter was in motion.

It's good to do things that are hard. Hard doesn't mean bad. Hard doesn't mean I'm stupid.

"It's okay, babe," Steve said. "Take your time, no rush. You'll get a feel for it."

And I did. After thirty minutes I could easily kick off and hop on the scooter. I started feeling more comfortable going faster. I got a feel for braking and turning. Steve was so patient with me, and I felt bad for being so grumpy with him.

"Sorry, babe. I'm not sure why I got so angry. I think I felt ashamed that it didn't come easy to me. I felt afraid I was going to get hurt."

The sun went down, and we scooted alongside the reflection pool on our way to the Lincoln Memorial. I felt the wind in my hair, I felt myself smiling. I was having fun.

I need to do this more, I thought to myself.

Yes, that's it! It's not that I couldn't do it—it's just that because I don't do things like this often, it takes some time to figure it out. Just because it's hard at first doesn't mean I can't do it. It just means I need practice. Most things don't come easy right away. It's good to stretch and learn and do new things. It's good to do things that are hard. Hard doesn't mean bad. Hard doesn't mean I'm stupid.

I remember how scared I was getting my first business license. I was sure the person at city hall would laugh in my face. Now we have a thriving business with more than a hundred employees!

I remember how scared I was being a new mom. I had no idea how to care for this tiny baby with special needs. But step-by-step we learned together.

I get scared when I need to have a hard conversation with a friend or colleague. I get scared sharing a new jewelry design with the world. On hard days, even going to the grocery store can feel overwhelming. Life is full of twists and turns, ups and downs, and opportunities. It's okay to fail. It's okay to be imperfect. It's okay to feel fear and step forward anyway.

I want to try new things.

I want to be willing to be bad at something.

I want to jump in even when things are hard.

I want to stretch myself and continue to grow.

I want to keep moving forward—and that means not getting stuck in one place.

I want to move this body God gave me.

I want to stretch my mind and learn new things.

I want to see new places and meet new people.

I want to feel scared and try it anyway.

I want to fail, get up, and try again.

I want to risk instead of playing it safe.

I want to be the best *me* I can be.

Fill in the blanks below.

I want to stretch myself and try

_____

One thing I accomplished even though I was
afraid was

_____

I've always wanted to try

_____

Think on These Things

I am not going to succeed at everything. I am not done learning. I am not done stretching my heart and soul. I am open to new things. Every time I experience something new, I get to know another part of myself. I am capable of amazing things. It starts with one little step, moving through fear, being willing to fail and try again. I am me, and I try new things.

A Lie and a Truth

Write a lie you have believed about yourself.

Now cross it out and rewrite it as a true statement.

BE
EMOTIONAL

*A*nger and sadness—I have confused these two feelings for a long time. I've felt a sharp pain in my chest and a tightness in my throat as tears welled up in my eyes, and I've known heartbreak. At other times there has been an awful feeling in my stomach and a tightness in my shoulders. For a long time I thought this was also sadness. I wanted to yell, but I pushed that feeling down and let the tears come. Sadness felt safer than anger. Anger felt ugly, and I wanted to avoid it.

I ignored my true feelings for so long. I would dip down into that dark place for a few hours, but then I needed to get up, splash some water on my face, and move forward.

Anger was something to avoid—and I tried, but it always came up somehow.

Steve and I recently had a big disappointment with our business. A project we had been working on for months fell apart. We looked at the situation from every angle. What if we backed up and tried a different strategy? What if we hired someone to help us overcome that issue? What if we started over and tried a completely different approach? As we processed and talked and worked through all the scenarios, it became clear—this project was dead in the water. It was time to pivot and go a different direction.

But first we needed to feel the hard feelings. I burst into tears, and Steve stood up and paced the room. "This is so hard," I said between tears. "This sucks," he said with anger in his voice.

I looked up at him. "I'm actually not sad," I said. "I'm angry. So angry." I felt my tears drying up.

He looked me in the eyes and said, "I'm not angry; I'm really sad."

Sadness felt safer to me than anger.

Anger felt safer to him than sadness.

Both anger and sadness were appropriate responses, but each of us felt deep down that our initial feelings weren't valid, so we molded and shaped them into something else.

Anger is ugly, so I'll feel sad instead, I thought subconsciously.

Sadness is weak, so I'll feel anger, he thought somewhere below his awareness.

There are no bad feelings. Yes, there are hard feelings, there are uncomfortable feelings, but there are no feelings that are off-limits. Feelings are information that helps us understand ourselves in the world. What we do with those feelings matters. While all feelings are valid, how we respond to those feelings may or may not be appropriate.

I've seen that when I deny my feelings and push them down, they come up somewhere else, usually stronger and directed at someone

There are no bad feelings. Yes, there are hard feelings, there are uncomfortable feelings, but there are no feelings that are off-limits.

else. When I don't recognize my anger in the moment, when I call it sadness and push it down, it erupts unexpectedly.

Be emotional. All those emotions you feel are valid. They matter. They give you information about yourself in the world. Sadness, fear, anger, irritation, nervousness, happiness, joy, excitement, contentment, silliness; we all feel these feelings, and they all matter. Feel your feelings and call them by name. Breathe in; breathe out. Give yourself time to feel without reacting. Take space. Breathe in; breathe out. These feelings matter. These feelings are yours to feel. They don't own you. They don't run you, but they are yours.

What is this feeling?

This uncomfortable-crawl-out-of-my-skin-guilty-not-good-enough-make-it-stop feeling?

Can I do something, buy something, eat something, say something, create something, organize something, run away, wash it away, sleep it away, or do something to make it go away?

I can't put my finger on it, but I don't like it.

Dark, icky, jittery, irritating, overwhelming.

Like a too-small wool sweater on a sticky summer day.

Heavy, itchy, suffocating.

It's swallowing me up.

I can't breathe.

Please don't touch me.

I might freak out.

It's all too much.

I don't know what I want.

I am alone.

Leave me alone.

Please don't leave me alone.

Don't say anything.

Tell me you love me.

Even when I'm not enough.

I'm enough.

I can't sit with this feeling.

I *can* sit with this feeling.

This uncomfortable-crawl-out-of-my-skin-guilty-not-good-enough-make-it-stop feeling.

It's hard to be human.

It's hard to be me.

It's okay when it's not okay.

It's okay.

I can feel it and let it pass through me.

Deep breath.

Another deep breath.

A moment alone.

Regroup.

Feel it.

Sit in it.

Let it be.

Let it be okay.

Please let it be okay.

Listen to your body.

What does anger feel like in your body?

What does sadness feel like?

What does happiness feel like?

Where does joy live in your body?

Fill in the blanks below.

I love feeling

_____

I avoid feeling

_____

I want others to feel

_____

I want to feel

_____

Think on These Things

Instead of striving, doing more, working harder, and trying to prove our worth, we can exhale, rest in the knowledge we are already loved. We are already forgiven. We are already worthy. I am a person with feelings. I don't have to rush my feelings. When my feelings come to me, I take a moment to listen, to feel them, to acknowledge them. I breathe in and breathe out. I am a person with feelings.

A Lie and a Truth

Write a lie you have believed about yourself.

Now cross it out and rewrite it as a true statement.

BE
NURTURED

*T*hink about how you care for your children. If you don't have your own children, think about a child you care for deeply. When this precious child was placed in your arms, your whole world changed, right? His tiny hands, her kissable cheeks, his fuzzy head, her baby toes, his long lashes, her button nose. It was a new, deeper kind of love. All of a sudden it wasn't about you anymore. There was a tiny person who needed you, who literally depended on you for every little thing. You feel this is what you were made for. You cuddle, soothe, cradle, rock, bathe, feed, and stay up all night for this precious soul. As they grow, you continue to meet their needs—planning playdates, preparing their favorite foods, helping them with homework, tucking them into bed with a prayer each night. Of course it's not perfect; sometimes you lose your temper, fail miserably, forget something important—we all do. But the bottom line is this: your child's needs are a priority to you. You consider how to help them grow physically, spiritually, intellectually, socially, all the ways. It matters. It's important. You love your child, and you want them to live a full life.

Now let's look at ourselves. I am a person, just like my child. I am a growing and changing human being with needs of my own. Somehow,

We need love and nurturing and attention—just like our kids do.

when I became a mother, I put my own needs on the back burner. I felt there was only enough energy for my kids—and I put all my energy into nurturing and loving them well. There are times when this is unavoidable. A newborn needs a lot of care and attention. It's a crazy, exhausting, beautiful time. It's unbalanced, but it's only for a season. It's important to get back to nurturing ourselves as well. Long term we can't care well for our children, our families, and our friends when we aren't caring for ourselves.

We need love and nurturing and attention—just like our kids do.

"No way," you say. "There's no time for that. Can you *imagine* if I cared for myself like I cared for my kids? That would be so selfish. That would be too complicated. It wouldn't work."

I want to challenge these thoughts.

There is room for you.

There is space for you to have needs.

It's okay to be complicated.

It's okay to have needs and wants.

It's okay to *be you*.

The truth is, you are here, you in your body, with your soul and your needs and wants. You can pretend you don't have needs and wants and that you don't need nurturing like your children do, but *you do*. Those needs and wants don't go away. They're still there—waiting to be met. Eventually they'll become so big and undeniable that things will get really messy.

Let's take baby steps toward taking care of you, nurturing your heart, and being a whole person with needs and wants.

A pedicure once a month is great, but that's scratching the surface. Not only do you need daily nurturing, you need hour-by-hour nurturing—just like your kids.

You need a cup of hot tea, five minutes of quiet, a walk through the neighborhood, a playdate with friends, a nap . . .

It's time to infuse your days with self-care and nurturing. You'll be better for it. Your family and friends will be better for it.

Say hello to your heart. Is it still there? Is it still beating? Does it still have needs and desires and dreams? Listen to your heart. Feel your heart. Nurture your heart.

Shower love on yourself as you fill in the blanks below. There is no right or wrong answer. Don't think about each line too much; just jot down the first thing that comes to mind. (If it's hard to be kind to yourself, think about what a dear friend would say to you.)

One thing I love about myself is _____.

It's really hard when _____.

It's okay to feel _____.

I might need to make space for _____.

I deserve a little _____.

Remember when I used to dream about _____.

A gift I can give myself is _____.

It was really amazing when I _____.

Why don't I take some time to _____.

There is a place, inside your heart, where you hold your hopes and dreams.

They were planted there by the God of the universe.

They are there for a reason.

They are part of who you are, part of who you were made to be.

They matter because you matter.

You being fully you matters.

Fill in the blanks below.

When I feel worn-out, I can nurture my heart by

_____

When I am tired, I can nurture my body by

_____

When I am empty, I can nurture my soul by

_____

When I feel unlovable, I can nurture myself by

_____

Think on These Things

My heart needs to be nurtured. My heart needs love and quiet. I take care of myself by nurturing my heart.

A Lie and a Truth

Write a lie you have believed about yourself.

Now cross it out and rewrite it as a true statement.

BE
OPEN TO
CHANGE

DAY 16

My role is changing. My boys used to need me right by their sides almost constantly. I used to carry them, hold their hands, cuddle them, and make sure they had snacks between meals. They still need me (and they still cuddle!), but it looks different. They need independence. They need to meet some of their own needs. They need to learn that they are capable and powerful. I need to free up my kids, let them go a bit, let them fail, and let them experience independence.

David, my oldest, has a disability. He still needs to be spoon-fed, bathed, and diapered. But even with his profound needs, he is growing in his independence. He has opinions, lots of opinions. He wants to make choices. He is learning to entertain himself and soothe himself. Helping him gain independence looks like letting him play upstairs while I make dinner. It's reminding myself he is able to come down the stairs and get me if he needs me. He makes his needs known. I need to let him grow up, gain confidence, and express his needs. He is seventeen years old, and he needs me, but in a different way. He needs me to believe he is capable. It's challenging and honestly counterintuitive for me. Since he was born, I have seen love as meeting his needs and

> Love looks like letting
> go a little bit.

being by his side. He's not so little anymore. Love looks like letting go a little bit.

Matthias, my younger son, is growing fast. Physically he's twice David's size, even though David is the older brother! Emotionally he is able to express himself better. Academically he's handling more schoolwork. He's maturing, stretching, and growing. Helping Matthias gain independence looks like giving him support without prompts and reminders. Last week he told me he needed to wake up at 5:00 a.m. to finish up some schoolwork. He is my baby, and I so badly want to baby him. I want to help him succeed and avoid failure. I want to make his life easier. I want him to be happy. I wanted to set my alarm and wake up at the same time so I could check on him and make sure he didn't oversleep or turn off his alarm in a morning stupor. I didn't set my alarm but ended up waking up at 5:00 a.m. anyway. I started down the

hallway to check on him and make sure he was up, and I had to stop and remind myself, *He is capable, and he can do this. It's okay if he fails. He can learn from this. He's got this. He doesn't need my help so much as he needs my support.* Love looks like letting go a little bit.

I am learning my boys were created to be who they are. They still need me, but it looks different. They need me to let them grow into the people God created them to be. They need me to believe they are unique, powerful individuals. And I need to be me. I am mom and I love being a mom, but I am also other things. I love to create, meet up with friends, nurture my marriage, and have fun outside of time with my boys. I can be me!

I can be open to change. My boys are changing. I am changing. The world is constantly changing. In the midst of change, there is stability. I am loved. I am worthy. I am me.

Fill in the blanks below.

One area where I fear change is

_____

One area where I want to make change is

_____

One area I feel change coming is

_____

Think on These Things

Change is hard, but it is unavoidable. I am open to change. I see it as an opportunity to stretch and grow.

A Lie and a Truth

Write a lie you have believed about yourself.

Now cross it out and rewrite it as a true statement.

BE
CENTERED

*E*very summer we travel as a family to the United Kingdom. Steve has family in England, and we love spending time with them. The kids have a blast; the adults hang out; we explore new places. It's awesome.

It's also really, really hard.

International travel means jet lag, and that's rough. When I'm jet-lagged I feel exhausted and grumpy, and I feel like I want to crawl out of my skin. I have a hard time feeling this way, but even worse is trying to care for David with his special needs. Even when I'm exhausted, David needs to be spoon-fed, have his diaper changed, and be given meds four times a day. When we travel together, David will be jet-lagged as well. That means he'll be extra clingy, and his sleep schedule will be off. Fatigue is hard. It's hard to push through when you're so tired all you want to do is lie down and fall asleep. It's hard to be a nice person when everything and everyone is annoying.

So how do we do it?

I've learned the most important thing is to stay centered. That means staying in the moment. Usually the present moment is manageable. It's when I start thinking about the past or the future that I begin to spin out. I tend to worry about the future.

Usually the present moment is manageable. It's when I start thinking about the past or the future that I begin to spin out.

What if David won't sleep tonight?

It's okay. It's all okay. Right now everything is okay.

What if our flight gets delayed or canceled?

It's okay. It's all okay. Right now everything is okay.

What if he gets sick?

It's okay. It's all okay. Right now everything is okay.

What if I get so tired I can't deal with his needs?

It's okay. It's all okay. Right now everything is okay.

What if, what if, what if?

It's okay. It's all okay. Right now everything is okay.

There are so many what-ifs, and it's exhausting. But the truth is, this moment is enough. Right here, right now, I can be in this moment and deal with the present. If I am exhausted, I can ask for help, get a hot tea, or go to the bathroom for five minutes for some deep breathing.

I repeat to myself, "It's okay. It's all okay. Right now everything is okay."

I don't know what the future holds. I don't know what if, but I know what is.

What is, is okay.

What is, is manageable.

What is, is here in front of me with resources to make it work.

What do I need in this moment?

Sometimes I need to cancel coffee with a friend so I can take care of something right now. Sometimes I need to cry. Sometimes I need to not be touched—I need space to be alone, even if it's only for five minutes. Sometimes I need a nap. Sometimes I need to speak kindly to myself and to remind myself this moment is enough.

It's okay. It's all okay. Right now everything is okay.

I can't figure it all out. I don't have to figure it all out. I can let go of control. I am not in charge of everyone's thoughts and feelings.

It's okay. It's all okay. Right now everything is okay.

Create a personal statement for yourself—a message that speaks to your heart. How can you stay in this moment? What words will speak to your soul and soothe you? Feel free to use mine or create your own.

_____

_____

_____

_____

_____

_____

Think on These Things

Write your personal statement down on a slip of paper and tape it to your bathroom mirror. Repeat it to yourself throughout the day. Let it calm you. Keep
speaking this truth to yourself until it begins to penetrate your heart.

A Lie and a Truth

Write a lie you have believed about yourself.

Now cross it out and rewrite it as a true statement.

BE
IMPERFECT

F or so long I lived my life in the tension of two extremes.

How can I serve more? Pour your unending love on your husband and children. When you're tired, lean in and give more. Be patient, soft-spoken, kind, long-suffering. If someone is unkind to you, turn the other cheek. Smile more. Keep the house tidy and fresh. Be beautiful. Have sex with your husband so he doesn't have a wandering eye. Be consistent with your children so they'll be well-behaved. Be like Jesus. Be everything to everyone.

How can I make myself less? God loves you despite yourself. Beauty is vanity—why waste time decorating or putting on makeup? Taking time for yourself is selfish. Deny yourself and your human desires. Pleasure is bad. Don't pursue happiness; pursue godliness. You deserve hell but by the grace of God you can avoid it. Suffering is good—it will make you holier. Lean into suffering. And remember you are worthless and God chose to love you anyway.

One extreme says, *I'm all-powerful, and everyone's needs depend on me.* The other extreme says, *I am nothing, a worthless worm who deserves suffering.* I ping-ponged between these two extremes for decades. One moment, I have it all together, and I'm doing *great*! The next moment, I'm a miserable failure who deserves to be unhappy.

Neither of these extremes is true.

Neither is empowering.

Both lead to frustration and exhaustion.

Both will inevitably fail.

The truth?

I am just me—in all my amazing imperfection. I am beautiful and loved. I am broken and tired. I am happy. I am sad. I'm angry. I'm silly. I love being with my family. I love alone time. I'm complicated. I love to have fun. I work hard. I need rest. I am a person. I'm not superhuman. I'm not worthless. I am worthy and loved—the God of the universe sees me and loves me. He made me to be *me*. He loves me just as I am. I don't have to do anything or be anything to earn love.

The truth?

So little depends on me. So little is in my control. I can exhale. I can live with open hands and an open heart.

The truth?

I can create a beautiful home and enjoy it. Or I can let my home be messy and order pizza. Either way it doesn't change the fact that I am loved.

The truth?

I can bring dinner to friends with a new baby. Or I can simply send

The truth? I am just me—in all my amazing imperfection.

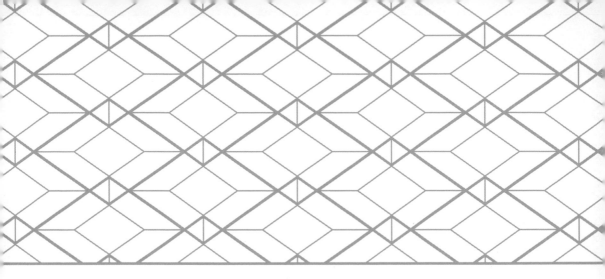

a text with my love. Either way, they'll be okay. It doesn't change the fact that I am loved.

The truth?

I can be patient with kids or be grumpy and irritable. Either way they'll be okay. It doesn't change the fact that I am loved.

The truth?

I can have sex with my husband, or we can say good night, roll over, and fall asleep. It's okay. It doesn't change the fact that I am loved.

The truth?

I can check items off my to-do list like a madwoman, or I can take a long nap and let it wait. It doesn't change the fact that I am loved.

The truth?

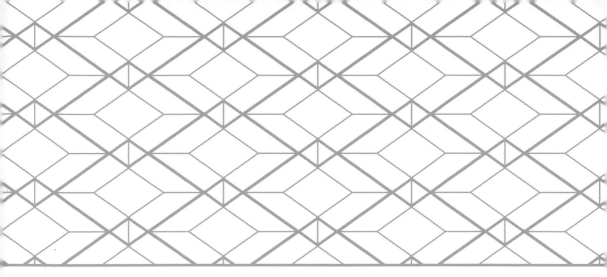

All the trying and worrying and serving out of emptiness didn't bring me closer to God or to my family. It just made me tired and eventually it made me angry and bitter.

The truth?

The God of the universe loves me, loves my husband and kids, loves my friends, loves *you*. He doesn't need me to be perfect and have everything figured out. He doesn't need me to be everything to everyone. He's got this.

Deep breath. He's got this.

Deep breath. It's all okay.

Deep breath. I am loved, right here and now.

Fill in the blanks below.

I don't have to be perfect, I can let go of

_____

I don't have to be perfect, I can say when I need

_____

I don't have to be perfect, I am allowed to

_____

Think on These Things

I am imperfect and that's okay. Sometimes I'm a mess and that's okay. I'm not all-powerful and that's okay. I am just me and that's okay.

A Lie and a Truth

Write a lie you have believed about yourself.

Now cross it out and rewrite it as a true statement.

BE
VULNERABLE

W hen we launched a new website for our jewelry company a while back, it transformed the business. I suddenly had one-tenth of the e-mails to answer each day. No more handwriting each order, no more sending PayPal links back and forth, no more paper cluttering the kitchen counter. Now I could go into the back end of the website and print orders, which meant less human error. It was a game changer for Lisa Leonard Designs.

The website made things run much more efficiently. Now I had more time to design and make jewelry—to do the things I really loved—and that brought me joy. I started reaching out to other bloggers, asking if I could send them one of my custom necklaces in exchange for a post on their blog. I would handstamp a custom necklace just for them, and they could share it with their blog community.

This was back in the days when blog marketing was very grass-roots. There were no big businesses using blogs to market. It was mostly just mamas who wanted to connect and share their lives, hand-made products, and creative ideas. I had a long list of blogs I read daily. I loved scrapbooking blogs, decorating blogs, DIY blogs, and photography blogs. I reached out to each blogger individually to share my jewelry and connect with them. Once again, I felt vulnerable as I put myself out there, not only sharing my designs (and my heart!) but also asking for something in return. *Will they laugh at me? Will they think I'm ridiculous?*

I carefully typed each e-mail. I watched for typos and tried to be clear and confident. With trembling fingers, I hit send and waited nervously for a response. Then incredible things began to happen. These amazing mamas were saying yes! Women I respected and admired wanted to wear my jewelry and share it with their communities. It was humbling and so very exciting.

Not everyone said yes, but no one laughed at me. Most of them wanted to support my business. I am still thankful for these women. They took a chance on me. They believed in me. They gave me courage to dream even bigger. Having the support of the blogging community and Steve by my side gave me even more courage to risk and to grow.

When we live in a safe place, we can find ourselves stuck. Without risk we cannot grow. Without stretching we cannot change. If we cannot fail, we cannot succeed. If you're like me, risk is scary. Stretching is painful. Failure is something to avoid. And yet, if you're like me, you want to grow, change, and succeed. We need to push against the belief that we need to be safe and avoid failure. It's not only okay to fail; it's good! Failure shows us where we have opportunities to grow. We are allowed to make mistakes. We are allowed to give ourselves a second chance. It's vulnerable and sometimes terrifying, but every baby step matters. Every time we move forward, we learn and we change our situation. Think about the life you want, and then take a step in that direction—even if it's a tiny step. It may be hard, it may be scary, but it's also empowering. You matter. You being you matters.

It's not only okay to fail; it's good! Failure shows us where we have opportunities to grow.

Fill in the blanks below.

It feels crazy vulnerable to

_____

I'd really love to

_____

   if I can be brave enough.

The first step I can take to risk and be
vulnerable is

_____

Think on These Things

I can risk and be vulnerable. I can ask people for something and let them say yes or no. I let other people think and feel what they think and feel. I can be me, knowing I am loved. I can be vulnerable, knowing I am worthy.

A Lie and a Truth

Write a lie you have believed about yourself.

Now cross it out and rewrite it as a true statement.